Genuine Black Woman

Keeping It Real

by

Jennifer Jones

authorHOUSE

1663 Liberty Drive, Suite 200
Bloomington, Indiana 47403
(800) 839-8640
www.authorhouse.com

First published by AuthorHouse 01/19/05

ISBN: 1-4184-5127-4 (e)
ISBN: 1-4184-5551-2 (sc)
ISBN: 1-4184-5126-6 (dj)

Library of Congress Control Number: 2004094703

Printed in the United States of America
Bloomington, Indiana

This book is printed on acid-free paper.

Table of Contents

In loving memory
Of
My father
Marion G. Jones
And grandmother
Juanita Johnson

Dedications

To Mama (Ms. Ada Jones), You have touched the lives of many old and young. Your generosity and kind nature has displayed such affection and purity among all of us. You have nurtured, scolded, consoled, embraced and supported my goals and dreams for years. You are graced with strength, honesty, integrity and morals. You are my best friend.

To my sons Michael and Trumaine
My daughter Lashannia
To two new additions to the family
Kavourise Damen McClure
Kiara Briana Jones
And Karen Artley

Acknowledgment

With special love and gratitude to all of those who has graced my life with love, friendship and encouragement.

Aurelia Wilborn-best accountant and (a genuine friend), Charles Lyda, (talented artist), Renee Carter, Janet Watkins good friend, Nellie Briggs, Larry E. Smith, my cousins Linda Jones, and her daughter Alyse Taylor Phelts Jones, Charles Jones, (uncle) Lovie Gantt (aunt), Herman & Margaret Johnson (aunt and uncle), Juanita Johnson (cousin) Gladys Goings (Godmother), Jimmy and Jane Johnson (cousins), Rosetta Pittman (cousin), Ruth and Ernest Dew (cousins), Patrice and Hardy Williams, Al Martin, John Kern, Doug Parker, Aretha Blake, Ms Mattie Sartin, Ms Mary Barker, Mr. and Mrs. Hector Allen (Best neighbors), W. L. Lillard (Thank you for one hour of television fame), Shirley Wheeler (invaluable), Charles Henderson, Kendra Reed, a great Business Manager. Iris, J.R., Briana, Alicia, Diane Howard and Danny Smith. Pam Jones-your friendship is invaluable immeasurable and irreplaceable. Your spiritual guidance, peaceful nature appreciation for life has overwhelmed me for years. I am so grateful to have known you, your friendship is authentic. Teresa Jackson, who's friendship has encouraged, inspired, strengthened and graced my heart. Together we have generated an energy that is truly positive. I'm privileged to call you my friend. Lorena Calderon Nungaray, even though we've only met a couple of years ago, I feel that I have known you for years. We have developed and established a phenomenal relationship that I will treasure for years. You are so genuine, sincere and honest. All of the things I seek and value.

Judnita Montgomery Smith, Richard Jackson, Rosalyn, Tamara, Phillip Pulliam and Maria Adams (I'm waiting for those awesome books), Reneie Cronin, Lori Hiles (Borders book store), Suzette McInerneco (57th Street Books), African American Heritage (Lisa

Reed), Afrocentic Books, Underground Books, Sirus Books (Hyde Park). Donita Thomas (A remarkable person).

My Poetry

If you are looking for your standard, simple style of writing
Guess what?
We're not on the same page
Listen up and take notes, my poetry mellows in your mind with age
I was told that my poetry was worldly, extraordinary, completely,
Neatly and extremely deep
This kind of writing will linger on your mind while in a sound
sleep
Allow my poetry to entertain you like your local cable show
This is all real, I just write what I feel as I let my thoughts slowly
flow
Forgive me people, but I must leave, on the next page is where you
can
Secretly meet me.
This is not a rerun, but coming to you live
If you need to obtain additional information, look me up in the
Jones Archives

To My Soul Mate

Your inner being has captured my soul and my spirits
You see, my darling you are love to me
How can I express such passion and strong infatuation
The universe revolves around our love
It surrounds our hearts as one
I feel through your heart
I hear through your ears and see through your eyes
We are bond as a new beginning, a passionate
Memory and an unforgettable present.
Our future hold an eternity of lasting love
And here you are, My man, my forever being
Of truth, honesty and character.
I taste your love, even in my dreams.
When I'm awake, I can barely speak
But yet I'm smitten as I gaze into your eyes
Once again I'm Hypnotized, your love is everything to me.
The sun, moon the light as well as darkness
All four seasons and for each one there's a reason, for loving you
The stars and the sunrise and sunset, you are my life with no
regrets
You are, words never spoken and wisdom never to be learned.
You are me, we are united-Today-Tomorrow-Forever

To
Jeffrey L Lewis
(Ominia Vincit Amour)
Loves Conquer All

Ms. African Queen

She's not phony, pretentious or immature
She is strong, stable and completely secure
With work, her family and her walk with the Lord
Her mind and heart are ethnical, she is no amateur
She reeks of beauty, character and integrity
Defining her attributes, to sacrifice and honor
Displaying a reflection of her ancestor's entity
Where she emanates a Genuine Love that upon her
She is graced with a delightful sense of humor and
Her ability to be outspoken
Is merely a fulfillment of her woman's intuition, which
Is only a small token
She is mother Earth to her children and a Princess to her mother
And astounding as it may be, she is love to one another
Her husband acknowledges her as his Genuine African Queen
And you shall address her with these words (Your Majesty)
She is elegant, voluptuous and portrays passion with each grin
She is observed by men of all races by the glow of brown skin
Eyes that twinkles like stars
Movie star-because my African sister with each and every passing
Day that's who you are
The fullness of her luscious lips
The curves that shape the contour of her hips
Her brows have a natural arch while her hair is worn in a virgin
twist
Her face is normally natural, today she speaks from the M A C
point of view.
She is the Goddess of her heritage, no man can resist. She is the
reflection of so many of my Sisters; perhaps this Queen is YOU

Your love fondled me like the scent of the ocean
I'm impelled by your inner being, you got me
Moving in S L O W M O T I O N

What's Freedom?

Is this what you call freedom?
Lacking all that is justified pulling us all down.
Do we need them?
We, in a bogus state of mind.
Since 911, our mentality seems like a crime.
When will it all end? In fact; how in the hell did it begin?
Not satisfied
But petrified
And to this, what a relation
Who's feeling the heat?
I'd say all nations.
We are still mourning the dead.
Only months prior, much was said.
Did we dare acknowledge the lives we had.
In the aftermath, we were left with a cloud of dust.
And to this day this horrific crime was totally pernicious.
Its way too late, to pretend, or insinuate.
And our children whose mind is corrupt by such terror.
Has a problem with insubordination, and this is no error.
And we succumb to the arrogance of a new person.
What we must do is initiate a pharmacon.
I ask the question.
How can one man out wit such a legion?
With an artifice mentality is accomplished without reason.
And we have displayed clemency and concern, for all of those
who has been deeply and completely burned.
And now, we are all in a war zone throughout the world
each and every hour.
And our leaders claim to have it under control
But only God has that Power.

Jennifer Jones

When I am dismayed my soul hears your soul
I feel nurtured as we reconnect
You have always been my soul-mate, with you there are no regrets

Anger

People with a hot temper do foolish things; wiser people remain calm.—Proverbs 14:17

Any fool can start an argument, the honorable thing is to stay out of them.—Proverbs 20:3

A patient man has great understanding, but a quick-tempered man displays folly.—Proverbs 14:29

Do not let the sun go down on your anger.—Ephesians 4:26

If you have been foolish enough to be arrogant and plan evil, stop and think! If you churn milk, you get butter. If you hit someone's nose, it bleeds. If you stir anger, you get trouble. For as churning the milk produces butter, and as twisting the nose produces blood, so stirring up anger produces strife.—Proverbs 30:32-33

A Ripe Apple, Now Applesauce

Waking up in heavens sight
He – to contemplate her tender young swollen lips and hollow
heart
His intense fiction floodgates, he has endorsed.
Which made her moist, with no remorse
An entrapment of his sperm
Once a ripe –apple- now applesauce
A loving soul – no more
Silent words scream
Only warm tears displayed
A heart once joy now dismayed

When the enemy comes against me, I will always dance and shout.
Satan is the least of my worries. I know God will work it out.

Arguments

A soft answer turns away wrath, but a harsh word stirs up anger.—Proverbs 15:1

Take care that no one loses God's blessing. Take care so that no angry feelings starts to grow in anyone. It will make trouble and many people will become bad.—Hebrews 12:15

Do everything without complaining or arguing—Philippians 2:14

Our kiss is sweet as honey and nectar
Love juices slowly running through my vein
I'll turn over and let you love me over and over again

Mary had a Son

What is his name?
What will he do?
She answered:
He will die for you
His name will deliver you
from evil, your sins and your salvation
The sweet name of Jesus
will heal a nation
His name will heal the sick and the broken hearted
He will comfort those whose loved ones have departed
When you praise his name
He will soothe your soul
Guide the young
and rejuvenate the old
deliver the alcoholic and drug addicts
provide peace for a restless soul
and cure any bad habit
He will love you unconditionally
Call his name, you will relinquish forgiveness,
Hatred, unhappiness, anger, negativity
He will bring you hope and encouragement
His name is Jesus. He will die for you

<u>And there was Mary</u>

<u>And there was Jesus</u>

     -cross
     -pain
     -suffering
     -blood shed
     -more pain
     -more suffering

-more blood shed
-death
-resurrection
-apostle
-Pentecost

Preach the word
  the word
  the word

Mary had a son, and his name is <u>Jesus</u>

I never allow myself to get into that male bashing
Respect and honest, is all that I'm asking.

I got Issues

Hey girl sit down got something to tell you, for this you'll need a stiff drink and some tissue.

I need to get this off of my chest. Cause baby, I got Issues.

Girl let me tell you about my job, don't mean to be a snob, that place is no fancy frill.

After I paid my rent, all of my little money was spent. Hell, I forgot about that gas bill.

It's rough on me, and I got a degree, but it means nothing I must confess.

Department of Education are not accepting fabrications and neither is the IRS.

I headed for my beater of a ride you see. Thought I drive to some place new.

But when I arrived to my car, I couldn't go far, there sat a brand new yellow boot.

Now I'm taking the bus and I run into Gus, who said he just got out of jail.

He said the system is no joke, I just missed child support and had to get a loan to make bail.

It obvious I'm dead, nothing else was said, he probably forgot he owes me money too.

I just swallowed my pride; I know he's hurting inside after all he's been put through.

Now I patiently waiting, but inside I'm hating. We stopped. Now, what's up with that?

The bus drivers on the phone and I'm a mile away from home, trying to get to a dose of Prozac.

And this sorry a _ _ man, I've obtain, who I can't understand is confused about what he wants to be.

He says stop hassling me about getting a degree, I'm happy with my GED.

I said don't mess up your life, you said you wanted a wife.

He looked at me and said what's the point? Its good you're concerned, but you know I've been burned, give me a 40 ounce and a hit off a joint.

So I finally made it home and I heard the phone. It's my sister and she's crying in a bind. She said that she was flat broke, cause she just left the boat. Sound like a client for the Payday loan line.

So I had a crush on this guy, whom I invited by, I thought this time I'll try a different approach.

Although I tried hard to refrain, but I was surprisingly entertained by the sight of a giant cock roach.

Now I got a new decision, I'm making some provisions. I'll cut back and economize. With this aging recession, I'm dodging collections, rumor has it we're going to downsize. That's why I called you over here, just to lend an ear. Lord knows I've been stepped on used and abused.

But Girlfriend, I'm tired, of suffering and crying, cause baby, I Got Issues.

Your smile felt like a warm kiss
Your eyes unveiled me, and the thought of your touch
I can no longer resist
Elated by your inner being, and the energy you bring
I'm far too satisfied
By a man of your caliber
Labeled at classified
And the mojo that you place upon me
Your heart gently speaking to mine
And the good lovin we made
Words can not define

Arrogance...

I will break down your stubborn pride and make the sky above you like iron and ground beneath you like bronze—Leviticus 26:19

Though the Lord is exalted, yet He regards the lowly, but the haughty He knows from afar.—Psalms 138:6

Pride goeth before destruction, and a haughty spirit before a fall—Proverbs 16:18

It is better to be humble and stay poor than to be one of the arrogant and get a share of their loot—Proverbs 16:19

Do not boast about tomorrow, for you do not know what a day may bring forth—Proverbs 27:1

Hold On

To all my brothers and sisters, who have been used, abused, lied on
tossed aside or abandoned by our system.
You know Ms. Jones if feeling you all the way. All of my love and
prayers are with you.
Try to have Joy, peace and always use the power of prayer.
The grace of God knows your heart, and promised to always be
there.
Disregard any and all aggravations.
God's Angels that lie upon you will give you direction in all
situations.
Material things will only provide a temporary fulfillment of things
you do not need.
When you believe in Christ, there is "True Joy," the greatest gift
that you will receive.
Trusting all that he has to offer will gain you the inheritance and
you will enjoy the Blessings that are sure to come.
Acknowledge God's Grace and Mercy and Remember the phrase
"Thy will Be done"
Allow God to change your life, to strengthened your character, and
he will give you the desires of your heart.
Accept God's only son our Lord and Savior and his love will never
part.

Aggravation from a system that has given us grief from the
beginning of time
Segregation taking our freedom our culture and any form of piece
of mind
Misinterpretation misunderstanding of our society which was
breeded from the same kind
Action taken only in the course of mishaps with each other
Satisfaction comes to those who can't tolerate one another
Subtraction committing crimes and placing them on our young
sisters and brothers

Hope is the Master of my Soul

Love covered me like a blanket of trust
Soul embellished by the inkling of time
A grandfather's clock with no face, yet, the hands of time still
prevail
The sea roared like thunder
With a midst of an odor
Soothe the souls, but paralyzes the thought
A resting place hidden deep inside the heart
A place of peace and tranquility
A place of virtue and integrity
A place of hope
Hope is the Master of my Soul
I see my Shadow in the moonlit ocean
It becomes by friend, but without words
I heard the stars thinking of me
Dancing to the beat of the winds laughter
And the distant sounds of the trees cries
Where in my heart is the crown place?
It has exalted time with charisma from the wilderness
And circulated the everglades
Now I asked the question
Are we all connected?

Jennifer Jones

If you suddenly find yourself thinking of me
Then you'll wondering why I went astray
Please remember I have not stop loving you
I just put my love on layaway

Anti what?

Dietrich Boneffer stood up to Hitler in 1933.
Trying to denounce Anti-Semitism which eventually annilulate millions of the Jewish Society.
Schools are a center from Governmental mind control.
Children are given the same rights as their parents
Apparently there has been a switch in roles
You can easily obtain a Satanic Bible in the public schools
But the Ten Commandments were removed from the school system, God's sacred rules.
Controversy in our Politics are not hard to find
Society diligently challenging all unchallenged minds
Lacking some of life's ability to stand firm through the prejudice of our nation
Contributed to the men of Demon minds, that contains unjustifiable contamination
Introductions to 'New Order', and "One World Currency", will soon arrive
Soon our Messiah will come again, Who will survive?
Your way won't be paved without the mark of the beast
Overthrowing all governmental policies with a Monetary Control Fleet
We are raising a Nation with the mentality of greed
Praising money instead of God, is a malicious addictive need
Heinrich Himmler was the leader of Hitler's Army and was trusted to exterminate the Jews
Pagan and Satanic belief was beguiled by this demon which was adverse rules
We must learn to be a servant to God and not man, for this world is control by corruption
Material items, Selfishness, Pornography, and Promiscuous are a few seductions
Some of the Constitutions and earlier Amendments are rooted in Scripture

The government is prohibited from confiscating your property is the 4th Amendment not just literature

But this country has stolen from every Nationality, from the Indians to the African Slaves

It is said and 'eye for an eye', and a 'tooth for a tooth', but Mr. Bush, empowerment is your game

Daddy Bush paved the way for his son without hesitation

Keeping this country in constant conflict, causing war between all nations

It doesn't matter how the American people feel, War is the sport to play

Sending our young people to fight this war to obtain (Oil), finishing your daddy's game

Preaching peace, but deep inside, it's a bully tactic which you will gain by this war

Ready to bury future casualties for your greed, is the ultimate score

This is America where votes determine your destiny

We're always experiencing economical disadvantages, Is this the land of the free?

Each day this country is being defeated, we've lost against Korea and Vietnam

Saddam Hussein is threatening Israel and attempts to conquer Jerusalem

And Kuwait's where the people who needs help, may see us as a lost cause

Other nations are controlling Wall Street, our country suddenly has a new boss

Our Regime has put their heads together to establish a Showdown with Iraq

For fear of Saddam Hussein powerful strategy of a chemical and biological attack

My heart is breaking so bad, for our country is sad, many are unaware that Satan is walking the Earth

But God's Angels are fighting each and every circumstances to demolish him and all of his curses

Courage

For I am sure that neither death, nor life nor angels, nor principalities, nor things present, Nor things to come, nor powers, nor height, nor depth, or anything else in all creations, will be able to separate us from the love of God in Christ Jesus our Lord—Roman 8:38

When you pass through the waters I will be with you; and through the rivers, they shall not overwhelm you; when you walk through fire you shall not be burned, and the flame shall not consume you.---Isaiah 43:2

Jennifer Jones

The noise of silence awakens me, only to feel the pain of yesterday

Mama, I didn't want to worry you

I know you can't change the situation
I'm dealing with this drama with patience
Each day I pray to God to ask him, why?
My momma had to go to jail for committing that crime
I know my daddy wasn't right
But why did you have to fire that gun that night?
And my stepdaddy (Nick) was doing well
Although you're in a jail cell. I think I'm in a different hell
Yea Mama, Nick started back drinking
He's doing all sorts of things. I guess he's just not thinking
Sometimes he come home at all hours of night complaining about everything.
Trying to pick a fight
He's constantly beating and scolding me at all times of the day
And at night while I'm asleep, he comes in and have his way
I know I am only 14 years old and being a kid is easy, so I'm told
Everyday I wish that I could get away
But Mama if I do leave, where will I stay?
I didn't want to bother you with all the things that's going on
But Mama, I'm trying to hang in there. I'm trying to stay strong
I been used and abused so much, till I stop keeping score
I thought about killing him, But I remember that's what you are in jail for
And I think about my sister all the time
After all, she's the reason you committed that crime
Shot my daddy for raping her when you found out that day
I was too young to understand until they took her away
I didn't know that she would loose her mind, took a bottle of pills to commit suicide
I know you was suspicious, unfortunately you were right
I just wished you would have handled it differently, we all could have left that night
I know you wanted to protect me from what was sure to come

We spent many days at our daddy's house while you worked that second job

I didn't know what went on at night

I didn't know her virginity was robbed

I know I saw a change in her, she stopped talking to you and me

I knew it was hard on you mama, our childhood you wanted to keep

And Nick was a cool guy when I was little, but my body I cannot hide

But Mama, you may have married a different man, but they are both the same inside

You know I'm not lying but life is hard and
My credit card is 90 days late.
I won't be denied cause I will be in line trying
To cash that government rebate.

Age found Me, Anyway

OH that's real funny
I looked into the mirror and all of a sudden there you were. A
Wrinkle
One small fragment that lie under my eye
There I see you at 35
And you had no shame to your game
You knew I'd kick, I'd scream, I'd cry
I felt life was over, I wanted to die
I was devastated, hurt, ashamed and just plain mad
At the fact
You attacked
The youth I once had
And I watch you each and every day
As you prey, on my heart, mind and soul
Like a game, a prank a bad joke
And you Mr. Wrinkle decided to stay
You knew I'd find no hope
I was just a mess-So damn depressed
You slapped that wrinkle upon my face
I feel so violated, humiliated, disgraced
But that okay,
It's okay
I'll be strong, I will hold on
I won't look back; I'm looking for better days
I will not be upset. Eventually I will forget
This awful curse you placed upon my face
Your game is played, and what's that?
Oh my God
Oh my God
Is that a gray hair?

Depression...

Why are you downcast, O my soul? Why so disturbed within me?
Put your hope in God, For I will yet praise Him, my Savior and my
God. My soul is downcast within me; therefore I will remember
you from the land of the Jordan, the heights of Hermon-from
Mount Mizar—Psalm 42:6

Weeping may remain for a night, but rejoicing comes in the
morning—Psalm 30:5

A fine sister
A handsome brother
His style
Her smile
A date
A new mate
Her Hand
Romance

Girlfriend, Please

Here you come in the middle of the night
You're driving me crazy, with this drama you're creating
See your Sista is trying to be polite
I know what you're doing, and I know who you're pursuing
So come in and lets rap for a while
I heard you were sleeping with your boyfriend's best friend
Now Girlfriend, you know you're foul
I just went through some mess with you last year around this time
Let me tell you as a friend, this Love Triangle you're in
You're starting to be a problem child
I don't mean to hesitate, but let me get this straight
You say you are secretly and completely aroused
Now I know the plan, cause I talked to Stan
Who also know your game is foul
Word gets around and It's all over town, that you are being played
This Greg has a boy, but can't pay child support
But he's styling in an Escalade
Why is it that everyone knows what's going on?
He's just spreading your business around
Not that he's acting cupid, he probably thinks you're stupid
For this new love you think you've found
Oh now you want me out of your business, well why did come here?
I'll respect your wishes and step back for a while
I talked to both of your boys, to them you are just a Love Toy
They also think your a __ is foul

A date
A date
A conversation
A new relation
A ring
A promise
A ceremony
A honeymoon

<u>Say Mister</u>

Say Mister; where do you think you're going
I'm sick and tired of you sneaking in at 5 in
the morning.
Smelling like cigarette smoke and some cheap perfume
Yea, I know you spent the night in a sleazy motel
room.
Did it ever occur to you?
I ran into your woman's husband Lou.
He's not blind, he know you're cheatin too.
I'm not gonna sugar coat this, let me break it down
for you.
I'm tired of your drama, Baby you and I are through.
I'm sick and tired of you and your lame excuse.
You dogged me for the last time, It's time I cut
you loose.
On your way out, grab those bills, cause you will pay.
Don't ask me, It's not my problem where you're suppose
to stay.
You should have thought about that when you was out
with Ms. Thang.
Lusting after a skank, forgetting the day our wedding
bells rang.
I'm through arguing with you, I'll see your a_ _
in court.
I'll let the Judge wipe that smile off your face when
you pay child support.
You sneaking around on me was the town's Joke
But baby the Joke will be on you when you find
yourself broke.

Discouraged...

And not only that, but we also have glory in tribulations, knowing that tribulation produces perseverance; and perseverance, character; and character hope –Roman 5:3-4

Therefore we do not lose heart. Though outward we are wasting away, yet inwardly we are being renewed day by day. For our light and momentary troubles are achieving for us an eternal glory that far outweighs them all.—2 Corinthians 4:16-17

And let us not grow weary in well-doing, for in due season we shall reap, if we do not lose heart.—Galatians 6:9

Euphoria

Words that echo through my soul
Interpret your desire
That won me over, like a hot brazen fire
No time for formalities
Only sensual and pleasurable realities
Don't disguise your love with thoughts
Render from emptiness and summit to intimate love that was
brought to me with pain
from your eyes to mine
A heart yet tender, a love warm and fine
This love is what I truly believe
You've got me opened and so intrigue
You've always been right by my side
Together, we generate a passion and love so strong it electrifies

A new husband
A new wife
A new house
A new car
New furniture
New Bills
Extra stress
His second job

Extension,-A Black Woman's Invention

I don't seem to have a problem with braids
cause this take me back to our African days

What once was our African tradition
Our ancestors are sure to miss them

(I too am a victim) of this new and ever changing system.

Extensions, Extensions, A Black Woman's Invention
To add, or cover up, what we don't have
all shapes, textures, colors and length
for you my sisters, I don't have a problem with
But these brothers, may have more to say,
They too are taken back to our African days
But remember, we're not disassociating ourselves with
class and style.
Forget the hair, and grace yourself with a genuine smile
Start accepting us for who we are
Excuse you, so what if we wear dreads, locks micros
Don't forget were all labeled as stars
Stop worrying about the hair, check out a sister's mind.
lacking long hair should not Be a reason to defy
We are diligently strong in all that we believe
and from this we all have achieved
a success story.
Oh, yes my brother, that is who we are, in all our glory
and to this day, there is no way
I can put down not one of my black sisters.
Love us unconditionally, and appreciate us, Mister.

He worked
He prayed
He worked
She played
Bills paid
An empty house
No dinner (again)
Her secret lover

It's Ms Anne's Turn

My Granddaughter who I adore
Is dating a handsome new fellow
But when I asked of her significant beau
She said "Grandma, Please he's Ghetto."
I set the brother up for an interview with my
Boss for a good paying job.
But when he ran into my Boss, instead of saying
"Excuse me Sir," He said Oops, my Bad Dawg
Grandma I've tried to get this Brother a job for months
I begged, cried and plead
He walked in trying to be cool
Acting just like a fool
I thought, now this Brother, I can't Believe.
Grandma, I told the Brother how to dress.
I said Baby, wear your Best
He walked in with Gym Shoes, a skull wrap and baggy pants
He had the nerve to place a gold piece in those pearly white teeth
I thought, Hell, This Idiot don't stand a chance.
So you see Grandma, he won't go far, he thinks he's a star
But I can do better than that.
I'm only 24 years old and I got it going on
I'm moving on with no regrets.
I'm an accomplish woman, with a degree,
I don't need nobody pulling me down
You taught me as a young girl, soon it'll be a woman's world
So I'll proudly pass my knowledge around.
So Grandma don't feel Bad, I know you want me to have a man.
But he's not the one for me right now
I'm living right, getting on with my life
I'll just be with myself for a while

ENEMIES

Rejoice not when thine enemy falleth, and not thine heart be glad when he stumbleth, lest the Lord See it and displeases Him. —Proverbs 24:17

If your enemy is hungry, feed him; if he is thirsty, give him something to drink. In doing this, you will heap burning coals on his heads.—Romans 12:20

You have heard that it was said, an eye for an eye, and a tooth for a tooth. But now I tell you: do not take revenge on someone who wrongs you.—Matthew 5:38

He worked
He's neglected
He worked
She's expecting
He worked
She's rejecting
He worked
He's suspecting

FOUND LOVE

I found love within the Lord
And the faith I have is strong
Though I may sometimes walk along
I will always be singing his song
I was looking for love in so many faces
Looking for love in so many places
I know now I was led astray
Till one day I decided, I'll pray and pray
He lifted my heart so high
And washed my sins away
Now I'm worry free
I know he's so proud of me
I found faith within the Lord
And his name I will praise forever more
Thank you, Your power is healing my soul
Your love I will forever endure

He's home
An elegant dinner
A candle lit table
Rose petals bath
His robe
His cigar
She's pregnant

Jennifer Jones

The Work of God

We will never manifest perfection. We can only achieve a higher love walk with God. You may excel with your own expectations, in certain choices in your life, such as career, education family, and social activity. We need to give ourselves more credit. Maybe we are not where we want to be in our lives, but thank God we are not where we used to be. We must look at our lives now and think about the person we used to be years ago. You have to admit, as you grow older, the more serious you get about your life. You become more focused, more spiritual, more compassionate, and to some, less judgmental, because after all you have just about heard it all and seen it all by now. Now you are ready to enjoy that wonderful gift you were given at birth. The gift of (life). We are what we create. If you didn't get the things you wanted as a child, give it to yourself now. Stop waiting, complaining, and whining. Gods helps the child, who helps himself. I have always believed that, no matter how bad things seemed. God always made a way out of no way. Do not let your past become your future. Change things now, live one day at a time, trust in God. The higher you go in Christ, the more you will achieve, and your hearts desire will soon follow.

He's shocked
He rant
He raves
He storms
A pistol
Some bullets
A gun shot
A gun shot
He's sterile

BEWARE

You better beware, because I'm documenting everything that
you are,
Have been or may become.
There's a lesson to learn in this relationship
I will not surrender, sojourn, or succumb
And don't try to play me for a fool
All jokes and games put aside
My mind, heart, and body will not be abused
I will not be patronized
And the way you and I met
It was a miracle it lasted this long
The way you were sweating me from the start
While smooching to a love song
I saw a brother so sure of himself
It really caught my eye
At the intense affection I received that night
I will never rectify

Forgiveness

You are good to us and forgiving, full of constant love for all who prays to you.—Psalms 86:5

Blessed are the merciful, for they shall obtain mercy.—Matthew 5:7

When you stand and pray, forgive anything you may have against anyone, so that your Father in heaven will forgive the wrongs you have done.—Mark 11:25

Take heed to yourselves; if your brother sins, rebuke him and if he repents, forgive him: and if he sins against you seven times in the day, and turn to you seven times, and says "I repent," you must forgive him.—Luke 17:3-4

Jennifer Jones

Your love mellows me like a glass of chardonnay
This passion is inadmissible evidence of premeditated foreplay.

When the waterfalls ends

Destiny has taken you away from me
A silence now beckons my heart so blue
A friend and latent lover, you become a lustful need its true
Now I holler your name
But am only put to shame
You no longer exist but in my heart
A deep endurance, I'll now part
But your love will live on forever
Your joy and happiness, I will forever endeavor

Jennifer Jones

Grandma's thought for the day

What's another Bush doing in the White House?
How did that Happen? I just knew Gore was a sure thing.
now the whole country's snappin (Got that from my Grandson).

FRIENDSHIP

Two are better than one: because they have good rewards for their labor. For if they fall, the one will lift up his fellow. But woe to him that is alone when he falleth, for he hath not another to help him up—Ecclesiastes 4:9-10

A new friend is like new wine: when it has aged you will drink it with pleasure.-Sirach 9-10

Friends always show their love. What are brothers for if not to share trouble?-Proverbs 17:17

Don't make friends with people who have hot, violent tempers. You might learn their habits and not be able to change.—Proverbs 22:24

Do nothing out of selfish ambition or vain conceit, but in humility consider others better than yourselves. Each of you should look not only to your own interests, but also to the interests of others.— Philippians 2:3-4

Greater love hath no man than this: that a man lay down his life for his friends—John 15:13

Repressed

Repressed Political Intention
Being a candidate for a con mans convention
Obstruction of Justice will gain you detention
If you are not aware of this fact, just ask Clinton

Repressed Nation
This is ligistics of a War zone, called the Revelation
Kowtow to a leader with an abundance of humiliation
We need a deliverance from hysteria into our own salvation

Repressed Sexual Desire
Our libido yearning with passion fire
Is it to the sound of Legato? Or Do you call hire Sire?
Are you making Erotic love to the mere thought of Esquire?

Repressed Sex Offender
Perverted sadistic mind that refuse to surrender
Grasp of a virgin womb so young, yet so tender
Now a permanent display prisoner of the Public Defender

Repressed State of Mind
Negotiating your principals impelled by a crime
Illusive Junta leaves your situation in a bind
Now the masquerade has ended, causing you to do jail time

There's no need for an explanation, and no I will not apologize. Glorifying God, is part of my lifestyle.

Forbidden

It speaks of hard grove and alleyways
A foul odor from a dead whore
Mutilated then capitated
Each slash on the body tells a grim story
A secret lover of many husband and some wives
A perfect 10, externally, but bare no morals, virtue, or dignity
Snickering comes from a crowd of ignorance, and cries from those
Who secretly adorned the victim
Many hands were dealt with in this case
Nine years of sexual pleasures, 26 years old to death
Unforgettable, Jealousy then death
His body bound with hope of a dark tomorrow
And the life of a gay past

Jesus my heart is lonely, where are you today?
Forgive me for asking such a foolish question
I know you are everywhere.

Living through my journey

I want to give insight and inspire you from my heart
Grace and Mercy are my friends of serving an awesome God
I've step on some stumbling stones through my journey over the years
I have to admit I've cried many nights, Oh yes, I've shedded some tears
I would not take one minute away from my journey
And the road that led me through today was rough
Even though we are in perilous time
Jesus knows when I've had enough
He will put no more on me than I can bare
His love and blessings will follow me anywhere
I do not look at the problem, but I look at the problem solver
Gods has my back in all situations, all I do is praise my heavenly father
I stand here in silence, thinking, seems like I'm always going through
But God came to me one day and said "Child allow me to use you"
Don't worry what people are saying, don't let their judgment offend
My blessing that will shine upon your heart, will put that to an end

Generosity

Be generous, and you will be prosperous. Help others, and you will be helped.—Proverbs 11:25

When you give a feast, invite the poor, the maimed, the lame, the blind, and you will be blessed, because they cannot repay you. You will be repaid at the resurrection of the just.—Luke 14:13-14

We must not get tired of doing good things. If we do not stop doing them we will get something back when the right times comes.
—Galatians 6:9

To be the replica of Dr. Martin Luther King
To celebrate New Years day with cornbread and black eye peas
To be the Master of All trades and be so called (Jack)
To sink so deep into submission of lust like an alpha deciae

Mississippi Past

Isn't this surreal
Life damaged by hate that kills
All the future hope that a child should feel
But not for the young boy named Emmitt Till

Snatched from his home in the middle of the night
Badly beaten by the men of the color (white)
No sense in fighting, you're overpowered by hate and might
Hung and found in the river, what was your right?

Face badly beaten, looked like a horror show
With an open casket displayed, so the whole world would know
And the mother who bravely shined as her tears from pain flow
It was time to make a change, we'll never let this go

And the men who committed this crime, never spent a day in jail
But that's okay, their day is coming, an eternity in hell.

Me and Jack go Way Back

I haven't been with you for a while
It will be so good to feel that warm smile
I remember all the nights, you listened to me
When I was depressed and couldn't sleep
Remember when we went out and got into that fight
Just being together made us cocky that night.
And the day I accidentally fell down the stairs.
Friends said it happened because you were there.
You were there with me, when my boyfriend and I fell out.
You were so warm and understanding, you are my friend without a
doubt
I was so obsessed with you, I nearly lost my job
So what who needs them anyway? They are all a bunch of snobs.
They don't know anything about our relationship.
I enjoy your company these days, you're whom I chose to be with
They tell me to get myself together, and straightened up my act.
Truth is I can't make it without you, I really need you Jack.
I got a call from my ex begging me to stay away from you.
So I lied and said I would, he don't have to know the truth
People are putting us down all the time.
But I'm staying with you Jack, a good friend is hard to find.
Don't worry I'm not leaving you. You, I will always defend.
If anyone ask I'll tell them the truth.
Meet (Jack Daniel's), my longtime loyal friend.

When the enemy comes against me. I will dance and shout..
Satan is the least of my worries. I know God will work it out.

Gossip

A perverse man stirs up dissensions, and a gossip separates close friends.—Proverbs 16:28

He who goes about as a table bearer reveals secrets, but he who is trustworthy in spirit keeps a thing hidden.—Proverbs 11:13

Anyone who spreads gossip is a fool.—Proverbs 10:18

Let none of you suffer as a murderer, or as a thief, or as an evildoer, or as a busybody in other men's matter.—1 Peter 4:15

It was a strong race between the Republicans and Democrats,
Yeah, they got over on us, like a fat rat.

Friendless Speak

I'm feeling everyone's pain
And it so intense
It's getting harder to stay sane
Is it time for me to slip away?
The hurt pulls me back again
Could someone give me a solution
Where are you my friend?
Why did we have to end?
When you left I was broken hearted
I've missed you deeply
Since you departed
Your untimely death has sadden me
Since you left
The power of God's Love
Has kept me glowing
And all my energy flowing
I wish I knew where you were going
I feel all of your love
Each time the wind is blowing

Dedicated to my father: Marion G. Jones

I've learned to praise God in the midst of the storm.
Don't pass judgment on me, I may praise him until dawn.

Attitude

Ever since he left
all you do is brood
I'm getting tired of you and
your screwed up <u>Attitude</u>

When you were together
He only give you the Blues
It was brought to his attention
If he snooze, he loose.

I know he broke your heart
I know you're feeling used
where is he now you ask?
I haven't got a clue
He's probably with the other chick
who works in the House of Blues
you gave him all your lovin
and he broke all of the rules
It's all over town
He made you look like a fool
now you are calling all the shots
re-establish your virtue
stop all of this nonsense
Let me tell you what to do
I know your soul mate is coming
who only has eyes for you.
Don't throw in the towel, please
don't say you're through
Don't give up on the Magic of Love
you might be a bride in June.

Grief

Sorrow is better than laughter; it may sadden your face, but it sharpens your understanding.—Ecclesiastes 7:3

My comfort in my suffering is this: your promise preserves my life—Psalms 119:50

He heals the brokenhearted and binds up their wounds.—Psalms 147:3

Shout for joy, o heavens! And rejoice, o earth! Break forth into joyful shouting, o mountains! For the Lord has comforted His people and will have compassion on His afflicted.—Isaiah 49:13

Happy are those who mourn: God will comfort them!-Matthew 5:4

Many night I wept, I was so broken hearted and in so much pain, It was a chore just to breathe. But I over came each and every obstacle, maintaining some form of sanity. Please, people say that you're feeling me.

Today, Who's This Woman

Crooning a melody on Chicago's Busy Street
Reminiscing of collards, cornbread and sweet meat.
After all, we're having a ball with a game of Bid Whiz
And Grandma's house, cleanest one on the block
We were harmonizing to some BB King
My Grandma still scream, at that man's voice, playing all night
And we don't have a choice, but to enjoy that smirk on
her ageless face
Maybe to you it's old, but in our mind her glow is laced,
With love and grace
And her teeth were white as snow, now a toast color, due
To all that tobacco
I guess, but let me put your mind to rest
She stayed strong as a mule
So don't you be fooled when she slip and broke her hip
She was just being cool
Hanging with her Grand chil-ren she was still saying
And this is all true
Although it is now 2002
And our English, maybe too far advanced for her
But who's keeping score
When you've reached the Age of 84
We knew what she was trying to say
And we adored her anyway
And she was strong in her being
Our way of enjoying her, is just believing,
in her Spirit that lie upon us.
And the things she used to do and say
Grandma we all love you and miss you, with each
And every passing day

God say: I AM

I read that studies show the happier you are with yourself, the happier you will be with everyone else. Treat yourself like a good friend. Women tend to be very critical of themselves. When you are happy, you attract helpful people and great opportunities say happiness expert, Saundra Anne Taylor. She states that if you go about your life thinking good thoughts, good things will happen to you.

There are people who do not know how to share themselves, their thoughts and feelings to build strong personal relationships, due to past experiences of getting burned.

There is no doubt that we are in the last days. In the Bible it teaches us that we will become more and more self-centered. Because we are in perilous times the world is getting colder by the minute. The enemy is busy. He is separating relationships to weaken them and to put them under attack. The enemy loves it when we are in constant conflict with our relationships. His plan is to divide and conquer, but it is God's plan for us to live a happy and prosperous life. Christians must learn to have a strong commitment to the Lord above everything else. God is always with us. We are one with God. The biggest mistake we make in our lives is worrying about what someone else is wanting, being, doing and having. God knows what is best for us. We will have experiences throughout our lives, some very pleasant and some very traumatic, overwhelming even. God make decisions for us. Each and everything that has happen and will happen is God's will. Some people will escape responsibilities to avoid any unpleasant outcome. Life is about learning and growing. It is nothing wrong with desiring things. We have to learn to stop judging ourselves and others. If you are constantly thinking about what others think, then you are owned by them. Guilt and fear are also our enemies. Guilt is the feeling that keeps you from being the person you suppose to be. I read something that I would like to share with you. Its words move me so profoundly.

God is God
The Supreme Being
The Beginning and the End
The Alfa and Omega
The Sum and the Substance
The Question and the Answer
The Up and the Down of It
The Left and the Right
The Here and The Now
The Before and the After
The Light and the Darkness that Create the Light
The Goodness without End and the Badness which make the
Goodness Good
Gods Says I Am the All of Everything, and I Cannot experience
any part of Myself
without experiencing all of Myself, I Am All that I create
God Says
I Am, I Am, I Am, I Am

Reference: A Conversation With God

Downtrodden

Old wooden benches with children cheering screams
Broken hoops with empty dreams
Sand box filled with cigarette butts and broken glass
Broken down monkey bars, dirt in the place of grass
Hanging chains, that used to hold playground swings
Downtrodden sleeping near the curb
This is their home, Do not Disturb
Young boys rapping lyrics on the street
Humming a tune, trying to keep a beat
Graffiti art displayed on the wall
Strong smell of urine in the playground stalls
Sprinkler system on, but no water coming out
Kids cool off with a fire hydrant spout
A store cracked window with tape across the back
Plenty of candy to choose from, but money they lack
Some Mamas strung out on dope
Some Papas in jail contemplating parole
Young boys growing learning to deal drugs
Missing out on Mom's and Dad's kisses and hugs
Young girls learning how to prostitute
Gang leaders scouting for new recruit
Rats in the alley out weighing the cats
Gunshot in the distant, sounds like fire cracks
Women on cocaine, once healthy, now looks like bones
Hustling for money in the street where they roam
Homeless family sleeping in a boarded up house
Using cardboards for beds, with a thrown out couch
Empty beer cans and bottles in the alley way
Some are hoping and praying for a better day

Life meant nothing to me,
Since I met you, I am the lock and you are my key
Each time we're together, our love is so intense
Now that you're in my life,
It all makes sense
I wish I could turn back the hands of time of all the days without
you
This is not a fantasy,
It is genuine, authentic and true

Happiness...

Jesus looked at His disciples and said: Happy are you poor; the kingdom of God is yours! Happy are you who are hungry now; you will be filled!

Happy are you who weep now; you will laugh! Happy are you when people hate you, reject you, insult you, and say that you are evil, all because of the son of Man. Be glad when that happens and dance for joy, because a great reward is kept for you in heaven."—Luke 6:20-23

Listen Up

Sex, drugs, violence gambling and prostitution
Challenges we now face displays restitution
Don't ignore the fact of reality, it's real not an illusion
Wherever there is life, there is pain, I have come to this conclusion
Career, Money, Education, and Power
We're slowly diminishing and deteriorating by the hour
Racism has been known to put us through the ringer
Don't be pulled, twisted, and sucked in by that crap on Jerry
Springer
Incest, deception, heartbreak, rejection
Look in the mirror, see your reflection
Get on your knees, give God a Confession
Iraq and Iran
To late to take a stand
You know its part of the plan
We're being destroyed by man
Poverty, hatred and brutality
Trying to maintain a composed mentality
It's a slap in the face, but reality
Drugs, Wars, Gangs and perversed sexuality
What we need is a massive antidote
To stop people from drinking, smoking, and gambling at the boat
A confused and misguided United States
Whom our enemies love to hate
Though they call this the freedom place
It's the truth but a slap in the face
It's a known fact that more men are in jail than in school
Oh no, this is not etiquette, tasteful, or cool
They are put in a place where the funding is easy
But not funded for Education, which I find displeasing
Their life is mapped out tucked away in a cell
That are full of horror stories of the living hell
Mind blowing, mind boggling, but it's a known fact

They can't get their past, present, or their future back
Black man stand up and state your claim
Don't give in to the possibilities of wanting life's fame
To get there you sell drugs, steal, rape and rob us of our glory
You can have a good life if you just change your story
And the ending will be pending of a world fill with glory
Put on a suit and tie and hold your head up high
And be faithful and grateful till the day you die
Stand by your mate, raise your family and respect everyone you
bestow
You'll be known as a good man with the love that your show
Don't be clinching, forget about the lynching
Go on with life if you can
And forever, you'll endeavor as a promising black man
Hate crime excursions
Sexual perversion
Gang leaders slowing merging
Lets handle our business, its urgent
Arabs, Asians, Europeans and Chinese
They're building up their business and we're quietly suffering on
our knees
Lets face the fact and realize
More and more companies will downsize
Its getting harder and harder to survive
Maintaining sanity to stay alive
I'm sure we're all waiting to exhale
Let's not get discouraged or we'll fail
Its our duty, lets not expel
All of God's children is catching hell

Pay your bills, make a will
Dominate your own mortality
Forgive all those who misused you
Contemplate tomorrows agenda
To an unknown reality, you'll surrender

A Grandmother's Life

Time put some pounds on me
And gathered some gray hairs
Hands like a leaf in its last stage
Voice that was once soft and supple
Has become deep and raspy
That star I once wished upon at night
Finally finds me with bifocals after
Years of shining
Memories of child hood pranks and friends
Whom I miss dearly
I have survived tragedies, loss love ones, and sickness
I have been someone's, Mother, lover, sister, daughter,
Aunt, cousin, and a very good friend to many
All of my insecurities, jealousy, loneliness, struggles
For a better tomorrow, are locked in a box of a
Younger past
I've been through childhood, marriage, childbirth, surgery,
Menopause, hair loss, ache bones, wrinkles, and dentures
I am self sufficient, self-reliable, and honest
I have surpassed all of the physical attributes for years as
I've changed over the years in appearance
After years of changing and rearranging myself,
I have been accepted, approved, and refined by (ME)

Why?

When did living get this bad?
Everyday is a struggle
Is this my last day?
You ask yourself
My life, What is it worth?
Everyday as I watch T.V.
I am disgusted and horribly displeased
All of the violence, murder, sexuality, abuse
Prostitution, hate crimes, extortion, drug use
I can't believe this world is in such chaos
Is it getting better? You know its not
And our children, Why are they disappearing?
Incest, rape, molestation
That's all we're hearing
Children, I have always thought were a gift from God
I believe these horrific crimes comes from those without a heart

<u>The Wild Card</u> says <u>I got this</u>

The wall cried as the blood scattered against its surface.
Cried of hatred, then freedom
Awaked by a devious need
A need to be--just to be
to be strong, sensibly sexy, sensuous, sensational
But instead seemingly slick sleeping in a slum
And all the time, she keep saying
Don't be pissed--I got this

With every awaken hour
she manipulate her womanly power
what happened to that young virgin flower?
Manifested with lust and the hate to devour
Keep dreaming sister. She tells herself, you are a survivor
Don't let them make you out to be a liar.

Devious thoughts creep into your brain
God please let me live once again
Her young body will put an old woman to shame
If pleasure is your game, then the Wild Card is her name.
What about Love?
Love has ditched a diva with distrust, dishonesty, distress,
disturbed by distinctness--No love here

I-I am the Wild Card

Show me what you've got and I'll call the shots
I'm the wild card, and I aim to please
stand up, lie down, or on my knees
do what it take to fulfill your need
Saturate your Loins till it bleed
me-I'm the wild card - Don't be pissed -I got this

Up until today someone fail to pay
Now this business – this business – is not for play
See there is a reputation involved
I go down baby - we all fall
This is a high price sexual ring
My girls range from 13 to 16
We rake in all of the cash
and you pay extra if we give up the A_ _
This Job is a business and I must survive
I have to do what I have to do
Hand me my 45

I been running the streets since I was ten
At 18, I can retire, I'm putting all this to an end
once again I got to take somebody out
It's time to play your hand - I'll show you what
the Wild Cards about
But in the midst of it all, there was another show down
this time the shot that was made was for the Wild Card
quickly the word got around.
Here was a woman In denial and delusion
Once so prim prose proper persuaded by
promiscuity has passed
The last words that was heard was – Don't be pissed, I got this.

Hardship...

I lift up my eyes to hills. From whence does my help come? My help comes form the Lord, who made heaven and earth.—Psalms 121:1-2

I will be glad and rejoice because of your constant love. You see my suffering; you know my trouble.—Psalms 31:7

Just lingering on Loves new high
Massively and passively loving my guy
Don't you dare ask me the question, WHY?

Its All Over

A body lie still with a cold empty stare
Its hard to believe only moments, I was once there
Now I'm going over my life, the mistakes I made, What could I
have done that would have prevented such a tragic end?
My friends, family and associates, will miss my company
I love each and everyone of them wholeheartedly and completely
My past memories feels like yesterday
I'm seeing my mom and dad as a young couple
I'm going through my life fast as the speed of sound
Experiencing good days and those of trouble
I feel the four seasons
Sun, hail, snow sleet, fog
Feeling good when the sun shines.
And feeling calm when its dark
I'm feeling emotions
So many emotions
Each and everyone of them so deep and strong
So overwhelming
I'm seeing the faces of those that passed before me
And I am wondering, Oh my God, Can this be?
This was my life as I've known it
And although life may be over for me
It was mine

Summer

I watch all the simple things life brings
The flowers that bloom and the birds that sing
Hollow dark night followed by sunny warms days
Squirrels searching for food, going along their way
I hear children playing in the grass that grew
And the trees with new leaves as spring starts anew
And moonlit nights so beautiful upon the river
And a cool breezy wind that will make you shiver
I watch the stars shining brightly, but soon to disappear
With a beautiful horizon of morning so near
And the mountain so still and the animals so free
And the fresh morning dew all around me
And the rivers and animals that supply our needs
Lets not forget the honey that we get from the bees
And our family and friends we will enjoy throughout our lives
And Gods precious love for which we cannot survive

Believing in Gods Love

God is always with us. Throughout all of our lives, God choose our good as well as our will. Remember the verse "thy will be done", Gods highest choice for him is the same as our highest choice for ourselves. We will always be one with God. God knows what is best for us. He makes decisions for our lives and we make decisions for our children lives. We do our will for our children, as God does his will for us. We must learn to trust and believe in God. Everything that has happen or will happens, it is Gods will. He plans our lives for us. God wants us to be happy. He wants us to reap all of the benefits of having a blessed life. We are looking for the answers to life's question. But we are given the answer each and every day. We simply are not choosing it. We choose what we think we want, instead of what we know we need. Some people have money,. They work so hard to get it. But once they obtain all the money they desire, they find that they are still unhappy. Happiness is a state of mind. We must choose to be happy from the beginning. All the things we obtain out of life is no guarantee that it will make us happy. If you have happiness. Then cause another person to be happy. Do it from your heart. Try to be totally unselfish and real with yourself. Give from the heart, not because you expect something in return. And do not give out of spite. To make someone feel bad or uncomfortable. The person that you are being spiteful with will get everything that you desire. Trust and believe in God and he will do his will in your lives.
Dominus Vobiscum (The Lord Be With You)

Reference A Conversation with God

Healing...

Being cheerful keeps you healthy. It is slow death to be gloomy all the time.—Proverbs 17:22

I have heard thy prayer, I have seen thy tears: behold, I will heal thee.—2 Kings 20:5

Jesus went around to all the cities and towns. He taught people in their meeting houses and told them the good news of the kingdom of heaven. He healed all the sick and weak people.—Matthew 9:35

Dear God

I've relinquish temptation
I've accepted the faith
I'm aware that you want me a different place
At first I was confused, evasive, misled
But then I thought about the blood that was shed
Dear God, How very selfish of me
Please accept me into your sanctuary
My heart was in turmoil my mind at a lost
In a dream I saw Jesus suffering on the cross
And so with this, you bared with me for a while
You captured my soul and made me child
I believe and pray faithfully that things will change
I acknowledge Jesus as my Savior and will forever praise his name

Corrections from Genuine Black Woman, (The Beginning)

Black

I am born black
I am breathing black
I am seeing black
I am hearing black
I am feeling black
I am experiencing black
I am knowing black
I am acknowledging black
I am loving black
I am asking black
I am answering black
I am working black
I have died black
Now I am seeing (white)

Jennifer Jones

Making black beans in a White kitchen

Inside my mind, I went back in time, and thought about slavery in
our modern world. A malicious and cruel detention and for some
of your well known text and history literature. Slavery—you fail to
mention.

I looked down and saw shackles embedded on my hands and feet
I'm tired of taking these beatings and the raping that was discreet

Slave owners saw dark skin and nappy hair and had no regards for
human life
We were all treated like animals, because our skin wasn't white
These white men with fire in their eyes, whip in their hand and
cursing on their tongue
If you disobey your "Masta", your body will soon be hung

Don't try to communicate- damn sure don't escape, death will seek
you no matter which way you turn
I've witnessed all kinds of affliction, but if you don't behave, this
time you will burn.

Crying out to God, why do you hate me so?
I've tired of being tortured. Please, Please let me go.

Freedom is all I really need.
Grant me that wish and let me be.

I promise you God I will behave.
Don't make me live life as a slave.

First I made a sigh, then my eyes started to cry. In my heart I began
to feel a hatred high

I didn't eat or sleep. I didn't even want to pray. I stayed mad at God for waking me each day.

I was taken off a musty boat and placed into a cage. My mind full of fury and my soul full of rage.

I knew working like a mule was sure to come. I didn't need to be agonized. Just take me back home.

Although, where will I go? My family was torn apart. I'll probably never see them again. They're a memory in my heart.

If I could just get away. If I could make a dash. I'm tired of that leather whip scarring my back with the lash.

Okay I am a slave, Will I get paid for the work I bestow? I dare not to ask the question. Cause my "Masta", will say no.

It's been years and years. I'm still here living the life from Hell. I keep looking for the promise land. I'm still waiting for the freedom Bells.

The Pin Cushion

If the Pin Cushion is your fantasy:

then dodging the pins are a stroke of luck

Each day without the pins are a blessing,

but there are days when you will get stuck.

Honesty...

Whatsoever things are true, whatsoever things are honest, whatsoever things just...think on these things---Philippians 4:8

Lying lips are an abomination to the Lord: but they that deal truly are his delight—Proverbs 12:22

Wealth you get by dishonesty will do you no good, but honesty can save your life—Proverbs 10:2

I just Wasn't Sure

My body contaminated with lust
From a man I was fooled to trust
Fingers laced with guilt on a so-called love trip
What was the name of that drink we had?
I know it was stronger than champagne
I think reason being, we wanted to celebrate
But I can't remember who I was with, I just can't remember the place
What words did I say? what things did I do?
What demons portrayed my body that night with you?
I thought I was only here for a few hours, but days have passed me by
When I think of what could have happened, makes me want to cry
I can't remember anything about that night, I wish I had some directions
Please tell me we weren't foolish enough to have sex without protection
I can't take it. I won't make it, you are the third man this week.
I'm tired of using loneliness as a crutch, and treating my body like a piece of meat
Henry or Harry, it doesn't matter to me, I mean what's in a name?
Each time I come off of my high, all I feel is shame
And now that I'm awake, this man I was with could have been a maniac
It matter to me now. I would like to know
I can't get those days back
This is it for me, I cannot go on
Times for me, do not have to be hard
I'm praying every hour cause I need a higher power
The man I really need is "God"

Jealous People

Jealousy is the rage of man; therefore he will not spare in the day of vengeance—Proverbs 6:34

Anger is cruel and destructive, but it is nothing compared to Jealousy—Proverbs 27:4

Love is strong as death; jealousy is cruel as the grave—Song of Solomon 8:6

HOW MUCH MORE

How much more can one person endure?
With a brainless occupation, I'm not so sure.
But you have to admit the pay is substantial.
And yes I'm grateful for not being financial-
Ly Broke – No Joke-
I'm trying to make it last
But time is moving fast
And my hopes and dreams are not yet accomplished.
And yes on some-days I'm stressed
But yet I'm blessed, in so many ways.
But this thing I do, Is not complicated.
And most of the time you're constantly stagnated.
To the fact, there is a knack
To the game of enjoying this occupation
Thank you for accepting my application
And granting me a decent life
To not beg or borrow
But to be strong to strive

Loneliness

Be strong and of good courage, do not fear or be in dread of them: for it is the Lord your God who goes with you; he will not fail you or forsake you. Deuteronomy 31:6

Though my father and mother forsake me, the Lord will receive me.—Psalms 27:10

I am with you always, even to the end of time.—Matthew 28:20

CAN I TRUST YOU?

TO BE A PARTNER IN CRIME IN LOVE WITH ME

TO SECURE ALL OF OUR SEXUAL INHIBITIONS
AND SELFISHLY AND ROMANTICALLY CONFIDE ONLY
TO ONE ANOTHER
SECRETS AND PASSIONS IN LIFE

CAN I TRUST YOU?

TO PURSUE A SUBMISSIVE, EROTIC BEHAVIOR
THAT IS UNQUESTIONABLY TASTEFUL BETWEEN TWO
CONSENTING ADULTS

TWO PEOPLE WHO HAVE MERELY LOST THEIR WAY
WHILE MAKING LOVE WITH AN IMAGINATION THAT
MAY BE TAINTED
BY WHAT COULD BE,
WHAT SHOULD BE,
BUT IS NOT

CAN I TRUST YOU?

TO STROKE MY EVERY THOUGHT AND WATCH, AS MY
BODY MERCILESS COMPLY WITH YOUR EVERY NEED

CAN I TRUST YOU?

What a Man

An idea of a good man is one who loves God
If he truly loves God, then he will undoubtedly love himself
Such a man is loving, caring, trustworthy, appreciate life and all it
has to offer
He is filled with joy, peace and loyalty
He is not envious, jealous, evil, vindictive, because love is not
these things
He possess admiration and respect for himself, his lady and others
If he doesn't have a face of a model, the physique of body builder
or the money of a CEO,
because of his genuine heart, he will be rich with Love

Love...

Thou shalt not avenge, nor bear any grudge against the children of thy people, but thou shalt love thy neighbor as thyself—Leviticus 19:18

Hate stirs up trouble, but love forgives all offenses.—Proverbs 10:12

Many water cannot quench love, neither can the floods drown it.—Song of Solomon 8:7

Love is patient and kind. Love is not jealous, Love is not proud and does not boast. Love does not do things that are not nice. Love does not just think of itself. Love does not get angry. Love is not glad when people do wrong things. But it is always glad when they do right-Corinthians 13:4-6

Love never ends. The gift of speaking words from God will end. The gift of speaking in different tongues or languages will stop. The gift of knowing many things will end. No, we know only a little, and we can speak only a little of God's words. But when everything becomes perfect, that part will come to an end.—Corinthians 13:8-10

Where God's love is, there is no fear. God's perfect love takes away fear. It is punishment that make a person fear. Anyone who has fear does not have perfect love.—John 4:18

Unborn spirits

Did you notice me when you walked by?
I was that pink cheek little girl with a twinkle in my eye
I was that bouncing baby boy with the clef in his chin
Cooing and gurgling with that baby grin
We did not spend any time in our mother's womb
Instead the choice for us was a vacuum tomb
Did you ever think that maybe we wanted a chance at life?
We could have dealt with the struggles of suffering and strife
But your selfishness took all of our choices away
You could have made it, all you have to do is pray

A child is born

As the morning rises
A child is born
Wrapped in flesh
But badly scorned
Heart beats fast as the time of day
A crack head mother
With his life he'll pay
Loveless and lifeless not knowing a single thing
Hopelessness and heartless what will tomorrow bring?
Addiction to a drug, for which he cannot understand
The future seem cold and grim and differently not planned
To hold him and see him so weak makes me want to cry
Praying for his life wondering if he'll die
Trembling uncontrollably as he cry out for help
His innocent little heart, I prayed for while he slept
Please make him strong enough to survive is what I pray
As the morning arises another crack baby on the way

Corrections from (GBW) The Beginnings

Old Age

Is not wisdom found among the aged? Does not long life bring understanding?—Job 12:12

They shall still bring forth fruit in old age: they shall be fat and flourishing—Psalms 92:14

Even though I walk through the valley of the shadow of death, I will fear no evil, for you are with me.—Psalms 23:4

Young people, enjoy your youth. Be happy while you are still young. Do what you want to do, and follow your heart's desire. But remember that God is going to judge you for whatever you do. Don't let anything worry you or cause you pain. You aren't going to be young very long.—Ecclesiastes 10:9-10

I have cared for you from the time you were born. I am your God and I will take care of you until you are old and your hair is gray.—Isaiah 46:3-4

STOP, WAIT

ALLOW ME TO TAKE A GLIMPSE OF LOVE
I NEED TO MELLOW IN IT'S ESSENCE

STOP, WAIT

ALLOW ME TO TASTE YOUR THOUGHTS AND SATISFY
YOUR CRAVINGS
I'M NOT BEING PROMISCUOUS
OR MIS-BEHAVING

STOP, PLEASE WAIT

ALLOW ME TO BE DELIGHTED IN YOUR TRUST
PRUSUE ALL OF YOUR DESIRES
CAPTURE BOTH OF OUR INHIBITIONS
WITH A LUSTFUL FIRE

STOP,

PLEASE

PLEASE WAIT

ALLOW ME TO ENLIGHTEN YOU
TO AROUSE YOU IN A GALAXY OF MAGICAL MOMENTS
WITH FORBIDDEN PENETRATION
OUR BODIES CHANTING SUBLIMING
HOLLERING OUT WITH PASSION AND LOVES
ANTICIPATION

STOP,

WAIT PLEASE

ALLOW ME TO FEEL YOUR CHEST
THRUSTING IMPETUOUSLY AGAINST MY BREAST
TO BE SATURATED BY THE SWEAT FROM YOUR BROWS
THAT FALLS GENTLY UPON MY FACE
AND TO FEEL YOUR HEART
ERRATICLY, ESTACTICLY, RACE

STOP,

NOW, WASN'T I WORTH THE WAIT

Patience

Be still before the Lord, and wait patiently for Him, fret not yourself over him who prospers in his way, over the man who carries out evil devices!—Psalms 37:7

Do not lose your courage, then, because it brings with it a great reward. You need to be patient in order to do the will of God and receive what He promises. For the scripture says "Just a little while long, and he who is coming will come: he will not delay." –Hebrews 10:35-37

Patience persuasion can break down the strongest resistance and can even convince rulers. –Proverbs 25:15

Hot tempers cause arguments, but patience brings peace.— Proverbs 15:18

The end of a matter is better than its beginning, and patience is better than pride. Do not be quickly provoked in your spirit, for anger resides in the lap of fools.–Ecclesiastes 7:8-9

Here is a call for the endurance of the saints, those who keep the commandments of God and the faith of Jesus.—Revelation 14:12

Seek God

It is important for us to keep our minds set on the Kingdom of God.

God wants us to seek the kingdom and he promised he will give us our hearts desires. He want us to walk away from sin. The desire to drink, smoke etc. God wants us to seek a new life in Christ. Colossian #3 Seek God. Tell him what you want and he will bring it to pass. God has patience with us. He knows our heart, who's trying and who's not trying. It is because of God that we have that good job, house, degrees, great ideas, businesses, fancy cars, etc. Remember him when it comes to helping someone. Don't leave God out of your pockets and pocketbooks. If you have a nice stack in the bank, remember who put it there. Even if you work an abundance of overtime, or a second job, or whatever you did for extra money. Remember who gave you the endurance to complete your goal. You did not succeed alone. The bible says Seek ye first the Kingdom, but most of us are seeking things first. He did not say seek things. He says seek him and anything you want, He will give it to you. Stimulate your mind and heart with his words, his songs, bible classes, teaching tapes and prayers as often as possible. Remember how much he loves us, and wants the best for us always.

Money...

No man can work for two masters. He will hate one and love the other. Or he will obey one and despise the other. You cannot work for both God and money.—Matthew 6:24

And he said to them, "Take heed, and beware of all covetousness, for a man's life does not consist in the abundance of his possessions."—Luke 12:15

When we were born, we bought nothing into this world, and when we die, we can take nothing out of the world.—Timothy 6:7

Those who want to get rich fall into temptation and are caught in the trap of many foolish and harmful desires, which pull them down to ruin and destruction. For the love of money is a source of all kinds of evil. Some have been so eager to have it that they have wandered away from the faith and have broken their hearts with many sorrows.—1 Timothy 6:9

Grateful love

I am you
You are me
We are nothing set apart
You can feel everything in my heart
I cry the tears that you feel
All we have earned
Was a lesson learned
Forgiveness is what we yearn
Hold on to memories of the past we had
Generation last
Present have
And the future, once so good, now seem so sad
But who are we to Judge
Our soul, our spirit, our love will touch
And if success is your game
Be thankful for fame
But please don't forget your name
Although it may not be your own
We have learned to make this life our home
Hold on to memories
Don't forget what you believe
I am you
You are me
We are nothing set apart
You feel what is in my heart

Temptation...

Watch and pray, that ye enter not into temptation. The spirit indeed is willing, but the flesh is weak.—Matthew 26:41

For sin shall not be your master, because you are not under law, but under grace.—Romans 6:14

You will never succeed in life if you try to hide your sins. Confess them and give them up; then God will show mercy to you—Proverbs 28:13

Let Me Be
(A Brotha's Cry)

I can hear the kids playing ball in the street
The ball has a rhythm, you know a beat
Beat 418 – the badge of a cop driving by
where my boys is somewhere getting high
off some weed, they bought from Pee Wee off the street
They be feeling good, in the hood minding their
own business, on Green street
Where me and my homies meet.
As we sit on the steps with
a portable TV playing Omarr Epps
Me be cool in every way
Not jiving, or profiling
Not sad, mad or even bad
Well, not today, anyway
Me be cool, taking it light tonight
While I wait for my boys
with some news about his boy
being shot yesterday
Yea, I heard he be okay
I can hear an 80's cut on the boom box
I got it blasting loud
And me, I'm listening proud
but not too loud, or police, will come knocking
on my door.
So I'm taking it slow
Me trying to keep a journal
Yea, brotha trying to write everyday
But hey, some days, it don't work out that way
I got heavy stuff on my mind.
In fact, this boy is way behind
With the latest news in current events.

Me been thinking, since the age of 12
While growing up, watching my homies
One by one – Go to jail- or even Hell
with all the crimes they pulled.
Chillin in the hood
Board with life I guess
probably should have learned to play games
like checkers or chess
If they could, probably wouldn't be in this mess.
Me be drinking, kool aid that is
Not that hard stuff
Man, you know its rough
My daddy drank and his daddy drank.
It's just one of those hereditary disease
With your liver and mind playing out
Hell, I just stay clean
Me be broke
Gotta little gig working 11-7
At a grave yard
Naw, it ain't hard
But my boys be trippin
cause the're scared of the dead
Not scared of a bullet, but scared of the dead
It don't bother me
I need that paper, so I can eat
Me be tired of your president, not mine
Him and all of those likes Him
Ask him something, and he will deny
Economy is so bad
AHH. its sad
Since 9-11 you see now, this stuff ain't funny
And the lives we lost
And all of those families needing money
But lives is gone, there is no cost
when your love ones lives are lost
I felt the pain on that day
Now don't laugh, I saw it all

On television, the whole thing and
I kneeled down and prayed.
All day and night, a brotha cried
As I laid cause I knew this world would be in a mess
Everybody was slapped in the face with reality
on that day, I don't think, nobody had a good rest
Yea, me be cool
Yesterday, today and tomorrow
Brotha, trying to stay strong, stay positive, not
giving in to sorrow.

Jealousy

Why is your girl so mad at me?
Do you think it could be jealousy?
Why does she roll her eyes when people speak of my book?
Instead of saying "Congratulation", she stand there with a look
What's wrong with displaying the talent that I have?
What wrong with making a person laugh or cry?
And telling everyone how much Gods loves you and me
Believe it or not God can't stand U G L Y
And it's not just me, but its happening all around town
People don't want to see you with anything, they just want to see
you down
And you confide in some of those so called friends you've grown
to trust
And you find out the hard way, they've always been E N V I O U S

What are you doing?
Where are you going?
Why are you doing that?
Worrying themselves to death like a panic attack

Just live and let live, don't worry about anyone else
You will find happiness in all that you do, just learn to love
yourself

Think Before You Speak

Stupid people express their anger openly, but sensible people are patient and hold it back--Proverbs 29:11

Blessed are the peacemakers, for they shall be called the children of God—Matthew 5:9

Let the words of my month and the meditation of my heart be acceptable in Your sight, O Lord, my rock and my redeemer.—Psalms 19:14

Poetic Disease

I have been hit by a poetic disease
Your ears will be entertained, your heart will be pleased
I hope to paved the way for my future creative peers
To be inspired and enlightened is what I plan to rear
I've allowed you to scrutinize my mind and fill a piece of my heart
You're not victimized, I've only improvised, you've encountered
the best part
Try not to judge me, insinuate, or even plan to hate
If poetry is your fantasy, then stop up to the plate
My heart is true, my mind is strong, these words are fresh and
authentic
I'm giving you a poetic experience that deserves to be commended
If variety is your taste, this book will consume you like an addict
You see, you've reached a sister with a vision, bonafide, satisfied
and ecstatic

Poetry/Self Help/Inspirational

If you loved Genuine Black Woman, (The Beginning), then you will rave over this one, Genuine Black Woman, (Keeping It Real). In this book, the poetry is powerful, honest, filter free and inspirational. This book will touch the heart of males and females, young and old. Genuine Black Woman, (Keeping It Real), is authentic, a classic and a definite keepsake. It is an endearing collections of poetry and essays that is sure to strengthen and guide. It will allow you to open your heart and mind. It is charming, witty, and immensely entertaining. It is a positive motivator that you will find both gratifying and meaningful. Jennifer Jones is awesome. A new artist with a refreshing upscale style or writing. Her talent is extraordinary and her creative words will mesmerize you. You will find yourself reading this book over and over again.

Upcoming projects includes: Genuine Black Woman, (Answer your Calling),
Poor me another cup of mojo (A Book of short Stories)
Evidence of Love: A book of spiritual guidance/inspiration

About the Author

Jennifer Jones is a native of Chicago. She graduated from MSTA Business College with honors. She worked several jobs as a Word Processor and Accounts Payable Clerk, before finding her niche at CTA as a Train Operator which she drove for 14 years before being promoted to Controller and presently working for 2 years. She studied Liberal Art's at Olive Harvey, St Xavier University, and Columbia College. Her Passion has always been writing poetry and short stories. Two poems from Genuine Black Woman, The Beginning, "As I saw the river," and "A Child is Born," Is featured in the National Poetry Society Anthology.

Printed in the United States
29963LVS00002B/451-549